By:

_____

Occasion:

_____

Date:

_____

YOU ARE
⟨A⟩

PRAISE FOR
YOU ARE A BLESSED WOMAN

"Women of today seem to think they are unique in their struggles, their dreams, their hurts, and their place in society. This devotional helps us to see that biblical women wrestled with the same things we do, giving us an unexpected *connectedness* that ultimately connects us to the eternal and unchanging source of help—God's Word."

> JUDY SMITH, State Director of Concerned Women
> for America of Kansas; Precept Bible Study Leader

"As you allow the Holy Spirit to guide you through these daily devotions, you will find hope, encouragement, and wisdom. Be inspired to live in an intimate relationship with your Heavenly Father."

> ALETHA HINTHORN, Editor, *Women Alive!*

"Dr. Martis Marie Jones has given us refreshing insight for our everyday lives through the eyes of biblical women into our Father God, Lord Jesus Christ, and the Holy Spirit. I invite you to treat yourself to a thirty-day adventure into knowing our Lord better and loving Him more."

> REVEREND SALLY JADLOW, Chaplain
> to Corporations

"Let *You Are a Blessed Woman* touch your soul as a woman and allow Martis's words to draw you into a deeper relationship with the Savior Jesus Christ."

> DENISE M. GODWIN, Freelance Writer and Journalist

"As a breast cancer survivor for three years, daily devotions played a major part in my victory. Regardless of what you may be going through, *You Are a Blessed Woman: Daily Devotions for Deeper, Richer Living* will encourage, uplift, comfort, and strengthen you, as it brings biblical women to life, connecting them with the struggles of women today. Dr. Martis Jones has truly been placed in the Kingdom for such a time as this."

> FIRST LADY EMELDA TOLBERT, President, Women's Ministry, Christ Temple Church, Kansas City, Missouri; Chief Administrator of The Lee A. Tolbert Community Academy Charter School; Entrepreneur

"Dr. Jones's devotions for this millennium will touch the heart of every woman who reads this book. In addition to a message spoken from the heart of each biblical woman identified, Dr. Jones has incorporated a personal message. Each day the reader will be led into a rich relationship with the Lord Jesus by worship, praise, and prayer. Busy women will discover that the length of each devotion is perfect and will fit into her schedule. Every focused reading, prayer, and scripture reading will infuse the reader with spiritual strength, inspiration, and motivation. More than one reading of *You Are a Blessed Woman* will lead to repeated enjoyment and worship. It is with excitement that I recommend this book of devotions to every woman!"

> DR. ALETHA J. CUSHINBERRY, Senior Pastor, Apostolic Church of Jesus Christ, Topeka, Kansas; International Church Organization Officer and Leader

"Dr. Martis Jones invites women of the biblical past to comment on contemporary concerns. Courage and hope are voiced for women seeking spiritual strength. Martis offers a personal application of truth for all women today."

> KATHLEEN MILLER, Ph.D., Writer, Educator

"*You Are a Blessed Woman* is a must-read for every woman. It is practical, personal, and powerful; overflowing with biblical substance that nourishes the soul. It causes one to arise to a new dimension in Christ."

> DR. ALICE M. LITTLE, First Lady, Greater First Deliverance Temple, Oklahoma City, Oklahoma

"The spiritual content and historical references explained in this book will give women and the world a better understanding of the roles they have played in undergirding the spiritual strength of nations throughout the centuries. The focus for the day and the organization of the topics give the reader an immediate connection to her area of interest. This work surely represents an inspired and spiritually guided compilation. This is a significant addition to religious—and secular—literature. The author is to be commended for taking this spiritual journey. I will recommend this book to everyone!"

> DR. ALEXINIA Y. BALDWIN, Author and Professor, University of Connecticut (UConn), Storrs, Connecticut

"Terrific! Dynamic and compelling! If you think it's just another daily devotional, think again. Readable and well designed, this biblically sound spiritual fitness guide gives everyone a life-changing experience. As a truly anointed vessel of God, Dr. Martis Jones has taken her ministry to another level. Women—and men—will benefit from this unique gift from God."

> C. E. PRUITT, Pastor, Bold Prophetic Ministries, Ypsilanti, Michigan

YOU ARE
A
Blessed Woman

To B Joyce Young,
You are a very spicial "angel,"
and I thank God for send-
ing you to "WOMEN United in
Prayer" and to me.

Trust and Obey!

Blessing

9/16/06

YOU ARE

A

Blessed Woman

*D*AILY
DEVOTIONS
FOR DEEPER,
RICHER LIVING

MARTIS MARIE JONES, Ph.D.

Best-Selling Author of *The Prodigal Principle*

WINEPRESS WP PUBLISHING

Packaged by WinePress Publishing, P.O. Box 428, Enumclaw, WA 98022.

The author and EdenNOW Ministries will donate one dollar for each
book sold to authorized, nonprofit organizations and faith-based
initiatives that service the needs of underprivileged and abused
women and children.

Cover by Ragont Design.

ISBN 1-57921-471-1

Library of Congress Catalog Number: 2002104794

DEDICATION

To six generations of blessed women in my family line who taught me, and continue to teach me, about the gifts of the spirit—love, joy, peace, perseverance, gentleness, goodness, and faith.

To my great-grandmother, Effie Morris Fields, who almost lived to the wise age of 100. She taught me about gentleness, goodness, and a healthy lifestyle.

To my grandmother, Beulah Arnold Fields, who taught me about long-suffering and unconditional love.

To my mother and bosom friend, Martha Rosetta Fields Jones, who continues to teach me how to pray and wait on God. She still exhorts me with "Completely trust in God" and "You can make it."

To my oldest sister, Patricia Jones Smith, who taught me the gift of patience.

To my niece, Felicia Sutton Wilks, who is devoted to Jesus Christ. She continues to teach me the payoffs of a consecrated, praying mother.

To my great-niece, Nieves Jones, who teaches me the gift of joy. She is bubbly and always abounding "in the spirit" of liveliness and laughter. At the age of five, she already knows her heart's delight—to be a "cheerleader." Everyone needs a "cheer" leader to spur her or him on and keep them motivated.

Also, to my beloved sons, Uche and Emeka Okpalobi. Uche teaches me to act wisely. Emeka admonishes me on acting with authenticity.

Most of all, to God, who continually teaches me to follow His will, according to His timetable. As I do, He richly rewards me with

YOU ARE A BLESSED WOMAN.

CONTENTS

Alphabetical Index of Biblical Women

Alphabetical Index
of the Blessing Focus
for Each Day

ACKNOWLEDGMENTS

A great number of relatives, friends, and church members kindly and generously contributed to the birthing of this unique devotional. A listing of all would consume volumes.

However, I do want to thank my four siblings: Patricia Smith, Vickie Goodloe, Portia Pruitt, and Henry Jones Jr. A host of aunts, uncles, nieces, and nephews in Dayton, Ohio, and Atlanta, Georgia, heartily provided historical resources and encouragement.

My Hebrews class, taught by Precept Bible Study Leader Judy Smith, continually exhorted me with "Hang in there." My editors showed vigilance and correctness in finding and fixing errors. This reminds me that God requires no less from those seeking to enter into His Kingdom.

The Heart of America Christian Writers Network critiqued my writing and gently counseled me. Leaders, workers, ministers, and supporters of EdenNOW Ministries gave their quality time, talent, and treasure freely and abundantly.

Throughout the wee hours of the mornings and the late nights, the Holy Spirit led, guided, and fed my soul with all sufficiency. I thank God.

INTRODUCTION

Throughout the ages, generation after generation, people have quoted Psalm 23, "The LORD *is* my shepherd; I shall not want...." Today, many quote this time-honored Scripture, yet few integrate it into their everyday lifestyle. Others use it when they feel they are "in a pinch" or in the depths of despair.

As a spiritual counselor and church minister, I hear people say that when they find themselves squeezed between personal tests and trials, it is not their practice to state or read Psalm 23. Neither is it part of most people's lifestyles when they are facing uncertainty and the certainty of death. Few see it as the answer to loss, lack, limitation, and loneliness. And even fewer use it as a confidence booster to discouragement and disappointment.

I have been teaching about Psalm 23 for several years, and it was not until I had received a flood of telephone calls after hosting a radio program on Psalm 23 that I realized how powerful its message could be. As I recalled callers' comments, I realized many people wanted to know more about how this powerful Scripture works to give hope and transform lives.

I was also encouraged to step up my evangelism of Psalm 23 when many callers cited how the compelling lesson from my broadcast encouraged them and helped them see they were not alone in their struggles. The testimonials and true stories I shared motivated them to take another look at the 23rd Psalm. This time, they deeply examined the rich rewards of faith, peace, and comfort it contains. Learning that God is always working out the details, they could begin to see a victory seed growing for good.

After hearing their praises, I began to reflect on the times the poignant passages had helped me the most. During my five-year bout with crippling rheumatoid arthritis, I was healed by daily doses of "Yea, though I walk through the valley of the shadow of death, I will fear no evil...." When I was recovering from divorce and a long, bitter custody battle, the words "I shall not want" prevented me from locking into a mindset of lack, limitation, and loss. And, "He restores my soul" kept me from losing my mind. Instead, I gained from a closer walk with God.

Then when I left the comforts of an executive position in corporate America to start my change-management consulting firm, I found courage in "I will fear no evil, for thou art with me." These tried and true words from Psalm 23 served as my sturdy anchor and solid affirmations of faith.

As I thought about other situations when my Heavenly Father, the Good Shepherd, provided perfect solutions for my critical needs, I began to ask church members, family, and friends how they were using Psalm 23. Most said to merely quote or read—not for focused application or a continuous spiritual lifestyle.

God broadened the borders of my tent. He showed me a greater ministry in Psalm 23. I was led to teach a broader audience how to apply Psalm 23 to their everyday lives to find true and lasting peace, comfort, and joy. I began to teach these inspiring messages and proven methods during seminars, radio broadcasts, platform speaking, and through the printed word.

As I extended my teaching on how to find answers to pressing needs, people—churched and unchurched—began to see the relationship between the messages and methods in Psalm 23 for healing, peace, comfort, and joy.

Today, God's inspired words in the 23rd Psalm endure as our weapon to fend off fear, squash doubt, and destroy discouragement. As people young and old faithfully use this awesome spiritual tool in their everyday lives, they discover that it works miraculously.

To the amazement of many, one who faced the full spectrum of the complex, human experiential mosaic—David—wrote the poetic and power-filled words in Psalm 23. A shepherd himself, he triumphed through the extremes of safety and peril, passion and betrayal, life and death, abstinence and adultery, peace and war, faith and fear, and covenant relationships and casualties. As he learned to build an intimate relationship with the Chief Shepherd, God Almighty, he found deliverance and victory from every peril. From firsthand experience, David learned about God's omniscience, omnipresence, and omnipotence.

THE GOOD SHEPHERD IS THE SHEEP'S BEST FRIEND

When examining the current-day relationship between the shepherd and the sheep, we can see God's providential care confirmed. The shepherd is the sheep's best friend. In fact, the best shepherds keep the best sheep. He is passionate about protecting his sheep and providing the best environments for them to graze and grow. As he diverts or destroys anything that could harm his sheep, the shepherd is willing to risk his own life for their safety.

For the sake of his good name, the attentive shepherd is known for keeping his sheep free from pestilence, poisonous plants, parasites, and other harmful pests. Because he knows sheep can get cast down and panicky, the nurturing shepherd keeps them lightweight and calm. Knowing they can feel fearful and helpless, he establishes a strong bond of trust. The good shepherd never leaves, abandons, or forsakes his sheep. They trust him and rely on his skillful mastery. They trust his goodness.

As their caretaker, the merciful shepherd ably applies the best oils to the sheep's open wounds. As he does, he calls each one by name and whispers soothing words to comfort them and cause quick healing.

And as he guides his sheep along each trail, he tenderly nudges the stragglers to keep them with the flock. When a sheep falls behind or is too weak to walk, the shepherd gently picks it up, holds it close to his muscular chest, and carries it as he continues on the path. No sheep is left out or forgotten.

The shepherd treats all sheep with love and compassion. As the intimate commune of shepherd and sheep journeys together from sunrise to sunset, the shepherd lovingly endears his flock as "the blessed ones." With the good shepherd's skillful care, the blessed sheep feel happy and fortunate.

WHAT ABOUT US?

Our personal Shepherd, our Lord and Savior Jesus Christ, laid down His life once for all, His "blessed ones." As our Good Shepherd who gave His life for us, His "blessed ones," He knows each of us by name. He knows our desires before we ask Him. And He earnestly comes to us so that we "might have life, and might have it more abundantly" (John 10:10). This includes all women, without regard to race, ethnic group, marital status, social status, or economic status.

Although the writing of Psalm 23 was attributed to David, it could have been any woman's poetic song of God's steadfast love, protection, and providential care. Even today, when applied prayerfully, it shows God's goodness, mercy, and grace. Not unlike David, today's blessed women triumph through personal perils of sickness, loss of loved ones, betrayal, jealousy, discrimination, terrorism, and war.

As women make the connection of contemporary circumstances to those in biblical times, they realize how down through the centuries people have not changed significantly. They are driven by some of the same motivations, wants, and needs. They endure similar pain, personal trials, tests, and losses. At times, they feel downcast and face doubt, despair, and discouragement. Through it all, the Good Shepherd continues to stand close by to deliver women and escort them to victory. All women everywhere, and at any time, no matter how diverse, share a common bond—Christ's unconditional love for all.

HOW TO BENEFIT THE MOST

Before you begin each daily devotional experience, set an expectation to focus on God and feel the presence of the Good Shepherd. Find a quiet place so you can give your focused attention to God's guidance. As you follow each devotion, tune your ears to hear His voice and listen as He speaks to your spirit. Open your mind to His guidance and follow His instruction. Soften your heart to receive His mercy, gentleness, and unconditional love.

Listen within as each biblical female tells you her story. You will find the dilemmas, downturns, pains, breakthroughs, joys, and victories to be much like yours. You will see how the answers they found match those from Psalm 23. By their true testimonials about tests and triumphs, you will be inspired and encouraged to keep pressing through your circumstances. You will find the fresh faith you need to keep believing in God's unfailing promises, find hope, and live in an intimate ongoing relationship with your Heavenly Father. As you devote your quality time, You will be treated well by the living, loving Holy Spirit. You will relax and enjoy His presence and power.

As you begin to use this *spiritual fitness tool*, allow your attitude to see each devotion as a delight to your soul rather than a daily duty. As you hone the habit of a consistent and regular devotional lifestyle, you will find it to be essential in these perilous times when uncertainty is normalcy. The daily spiritual guidance will equip you to build a solid foundation to support and maintain your daily fellowship with God. This will enable you to stay rooted and grounded in truth, bear much fruit, and enjoy more abundance. With God as your friend and guide, you will create your hallmark of victorious living.

Take time every day, in the morning or whenever you can, to carve out quiet time for your devotional experience. This will be your best treat for the day. It will help you gain clarity, find peace, discern truth, and stir up the joy in your soul. You will find ready-made answers and solid solutions to some of your most trying situations. If you miss a day, be gentle with yourself. Quickly pick up where you left off and continue on your path to spiritual growth.

You will find that each devotion brings clear focus to a proven practice such as faith or courage and can be read in about five minutes. As you earnestly pray about what you learned and listen for God's guidance, He will speak answers into your spirit. You will remember the lessons for a lifetime.

The purpose of the "Extended Scriptures" at the end of the devotions is to give you more in-depth insight about the lesson. You can read the Scriptures during your quiet time and in times of family Bible study, women's Bible study, or book club discussions.

Through the powerful devotional experiences in this timely tool, you follow a daily focus and meditate on the Word of God throughout the day. You will apply appropriate Scriptures to find answers that work, and you will find balance. You will create a lifetime of meaningful quiet time for inspiration and encouragement. And, you will enjoy freedom, peace of mind, and creativity. Your Heavenly Father will richly reward you as you discover

YOU ARE A BLESSED WOMAN!

Prologue

Welcome to your new beginning. This is the time for you to look ahead. As you do, set new expectations, choose new goals, and prepare for the unlimited possibilities God has planned for you.

Today, as you begin anew, thank God for leading you to this *New Beginning*. Thank Him for this new experience and the time to draw closer to Him.

Thank God for helping you turn to Him for your desires, dreams, and new direction. Pray and expect full measures of joy, encouragement, and peace. As God blesses you, delight in new ways to live victoriously and bless others.

With fresh faith, meet God in quiet devotion each day. As you begin, ask Him,

> *"Listen to my voice in the morning, LORD.*
> *Each morning I will bring my requests to you*
> *and wait expectantly."*
>
> —Psalm 5:3, NLT

Let's begin anew.

THE 23RD PSALM

he LORD is my shepherd; I shall not want.

He maketh me to lie down in green pastures:
he leadeth me beside the still waters.

He restoreth my soul:
he leadeth me in the paths of righteousness for his name's sake.

Yea, though I walk through the valley of the shadow of death,
I will fear no evil: for thou art with me;
thy rod and thy staff they comfort me.

Thou preparest a table before me
in the presence of mine enemies:
thou anointest my head with oil;
my cup runneth over.

Surely goodness and mercy shall follow me all the days of my life:
and I will dwell in the house of the LORD for ever.

—Psalm 23:1–6

THE NEW BEGINNING

SCRIPTURE
"The ..."

—Psalm 23:1a

BLESSED WOMAN FOR TODAY
EVE

M y name means "life." Although Adam was the first human created by God, I was assigned the symbol "life" and became the "mother of all living" (Genesis 3:20). My blessing of life was secondary to the absolute and perfect life—God, who is all-powerful, all-knowing, everywhere-present, the First and the Last.

God exalted me with dominion and gave me equal status with my husband Adam. Then He gave both of us authority and dominion over all living creatures in our homeland called Paradise.

I lived in an intimate relationship with God. As we walked and talked each day, He led me, guided me, and instructed me on the care and keeping of Paradise and the nourishment of my soul. He showed me how in hearing His voice and listening to His words for protection, prosperity, and provision, I would find peace, joy, and comfort. I would live a perfect life—richly and deeply—in Paradise. I was truly a blessed woman.

One day, my listening pattern changed. The deceiver led me astray. This sly, subtle serpent told me I could have more. I listened to him, not to God, the all-knowing Absolute Power, and lost it all—Paradise, perfect peace, a happy marriage, and my intimate relationship with God. Immediately afterward, gain turned to pain and innocence to blame and shame.

God wants us to listen to Him and keep a close relationship with Him. As He speaks, He asks that we open our ears to hear His voice and our hearts to receive His love. When we do not listen or willfully go against His instructions, He gives us another chance. Through His love and grace, He shows new mercy. He is faithful to forgive and is patient as we begin again.

Today, God blesses us with a new beginning. We can start by forgiving ourselves for not listening to God as closely as needed. Then we can ask Him to forgive us. There is no need for anyone to hide from God. He is open, receptive, and ready to forgive us. He wants us to only ask, seek, and knock. And then, He will swing the door open wide to receive us.

Ask Him what you need right now, and He will hear you and know your need.

PRAYER

Loving Lord, Absolute Power in all life, help me to listen and to hear Your voice when You speak. As You guide me to the right direction, help me keep sight of You. Help me to rely on Your ever-abiding presence. Thank You for life and love. Thank You for new mercy and grace every day. Amen.

EXTENDED SCRIPTURES
Genesis 1:26, 3:20, 4:1, 16, 21, 25:12–18;
2 Corinthians 11:3; 1 Timothy 2:13

BLESSING FOCUS
Women Facing Change

PART ONE
FAITH

ften we are too busy to see what is best for us. God, our eagle-eyed Great Shepherd, sees all and is our All in all situations. He knows our best blessings and guides us to receive them.

Faithfully, we can say, "Not our will, but God's," because His will for us is good—all the time.

Faith

Scripture
"The LORD is …"

—Psalm 23:1a

Blessed Woman for Today
Anna

Recognized as a woman of great faith, I kept an intimate relationship with God. As I prayed and upheld spiritual devotion to Him, He heard me and answered me. Because I allowed Him to speak through me, people in Jesus' early days trusted in my prophecies. It was almost unheard of for a female to speak prophecies. However, Jesus was called prophet as I was called prophetess, and I was the first woman to proclaim Jesus as the Christ.

One day, after I had finished my prayers, praises, and thanksgiving in the temple, I saw the prophecy about the coming of the Messiah and the reign of righteousness fulfilled before my hopeful eyes. Along with Joseph, Jesus' mother Mary brought Jesus to be laid before the altar in the temple. I declared to all that could hear me that Jesus was the "promised Messiah." God's prophecy of "the Hope of Israel" and the "Redeemer of the world" was fulfilled. I thanked Him for keeping His promise.

When we practice a daily devotion to the Word of God, we build an awareness of our faith, courage, and confidence. God shows us who He is and "whose we are" in Him. He mentors us as we groom and grow our spiritual gifts and talents. He shows us our true potential as we continue to grow spiritually.

As busy women, rushing through a fast-paced, topsy-turvy world, let us remove ourselves from the daily dictates of "must do," "have to," "yes, yes, yes," and "I don't want to, but I don't know how to say no." Shift gears.

Move into a quiet, peaceful place of prayer and meditation. You do not have to feel compelled to "do it all." You can let go. You can surrender your will to God's will for your peace and serenity. Even more so, allow God to speak to you and tell you when to say no. Also, He will help you to not feel uncomfortable or guilty. You will feel calm and stay poised as you make critical decisions.

PRAYER

Dear Lord, Provider and Keeper of my soul, help me to see that as I seek You, You seek me to stay in an intimate relationship with You. I look to You for all things and trust in Your promise to redeem me, comfort me, and care for my needs. Thank You for this evidence of Your love for me. Amen.

EXTENDED SCRIPTURES
Luke 2:36–38; Psalm 42:1–2, 100:3; Hebrews 11:1; Jeremiah 17:19; Psalm 139:23–24

BLESSING FOCUS
Mothers and Daughters

FAITH

SCRIPTURE
"The LORD is my shepherd …"

—Psalm 23:1a

BLESSED WOMAN FOR TODAY
PRISCILLA

or me to earn the esteemed status of one of the most influential women in the New Testament Church took a deep, abiding faith in God. This kind of faith was needed for me to serve as church leader in three churches—Corinth, Ephesus, and Rome. As I traveled countless miles to spread the gospel, I was spared persecution and stoning.

Well-versed and learned men such as Paul and Apollos respected me and recognized me as a bold, confident woman of amazing ability and intellect. I taught and preached, believing there is nothing too hard for God. In turn, He always supplied my needs.

Like Priscilla, at times we face what look like impossible challenges and unfamiliar circumstances in our lives. Our many needs seem too overwhelming to deal with and too daunting to describe. In the midst of life's hardships, God still sees us as His handiwork, capable of thriving through tough times. As we do, He keeps His watchful eyes on us. He never slumbers nor sleeps.

As we trust in His continuous provision, we can earnestly affirm: We are well cared for by our all-knowing God. He supplies more than enough for our needs.

PRAYER

Sweet loving Lord, my Provider of plenty, keep me faithful to Your enduring truth that, through Your everlasting love, I have all that I need for every situation. Amen.

EXTENDED SCRIPTURES
Acts 18:12, 18, 26; Romans 16:3; 1 Corinthians 16:19;
2 Timothy 4:19

BLESSING FOCUS
Women Serving in Nontraditional Roles

FAITH

"The LORD is my shepherd; I shall not want."
—Psalm 23:1

BLESSED WOMAN FOR TODAY
LOIS

eferring to me, the word "grandmother" appears only once in the Bible. As Timothy's consecrated grandmother, I took over his early childhood care. While his widowed mother, Eunice, worked outside the home, I trained Timothy and taught him the ways of righteousness and godly living until he reached the tender age of fifteen.

It was then that the Apostle Paul began to take Timothy on missionary journeys to preach with him and Silas (about A.D. 45). When Timothy left home, I felt sadness and loss. A vital piece of me seemed to be missing.

My faith in God steered me to what I had taught Timothy—prayer. God reassured me that the godly qualities I had taught Timothy—righteousness, love, meekness, and faith—would heal my grieving heart and renew my spirit. God was true to His promise that He would never leave me alone or feeling lonely.

As our children leave home to begin new jobs, pursue promising careers, enter college, marry, or turn "apron strings to adult wings," we can go to God in faith. Faithful, thoughtful, prayerful child training prepares our children to take on new responsibilities while acting with integrity.

As we teach them, children will model our Godlike example. We can rest in peace knowing that they will show kindness, love, peacefulness, and tenderness toward others. God will comfort our hearts and fill every need as He watches over our children and our households.

PRAYER

Dear Lord, Good Shepherd who watches over Your children and children's children, help me to keep believing in Your unfailing promises. Help me to prepare children to live responsibly and follow after righteousness. Help me to feel whole and complete in You. Amen.

EXTENDED SCRIPTURES
1 Timothy 6:10–11; 2 Timothy 1:5, 3:11–15; Acts 14:8–20

BLESSING FOCUS
Grandmothers Caring for Grandchildren

FAITH

SCRIPTURE
"He maketh me to lie down in green pastures ..."
—Psalm 23:2a

BLESSED WOMAN FOR TODAY
SARAH

was a part of two firsts: I was the beautiful and distinguished wife of Abraham, the first patriarch and father of the Hebrew nation; and the first of the four biblical matriarchs (the others were Rebekah, Leah, and Rachel). While I was barren, I doubted God's ability to open my womb. Even when God was telling my husband Abraham that He would make (his) descendants "as the dust of the earth" and that the whole land of Canaan would belong to his descendants (Genesis 13:16), I laughed at God. After all, how could this happen to me, one barren and well past the childbearing age? Acting from doubt and fear, I offered my slave maid, Hagar, to my husband. She was Egyptian and bore him a son named Ishmael.

Oh, if I had truly trusted God's promise! When my husband Abraham was age ninety-nine, the Lord told him I would bear him a son. Mind you, by then I was ninety years of age. In due time, I conceived and delivered our beautiful son Isaac (Hebrew for "he laughed"). As I lived to be the wise age of 127, I learned to keep my faith unfaltering and focused on God's promises. He never disappointed me.

The old hymn "Tis So Sweet To Trust In Jesus" is so poignant in times when the unseen seems so unreal or beyond our reach. The song admonishes us to take Him at His Word and rest upon His promise. Then, with simple faith, we trust in the joy and peace that God gives. Faith is the substance of what we hope for and the evidence of those things that were not previously seen (from Hebrews 11:1).

When you cannot see the end result of requests you make to God, dig your heels in deeply and stand firm on God's promise. Don't sell out too soon, compromise unwisely, or give up on the manifestation of God's perfect answer to your fervent prayers. He may not deliver on your time schedule, but He's always on time—His perfect time.

PRAYER

Eternal Faith Builder, my Lord and Savior, You are sovereign and supreme. I admit that my fears and doubts cause me to give up, quit too soon, and not trust in You. Forgive me, Lord. Teach me how to wait for Your perfect manifestation in the affairs of my life. Renew my strength and sustain my faith. Teach me to wait on You, for Your way is best. Amen.

EXTENDED SCRIPTURES
Genesis 1–25, 49:31; Isaiah 51:2; Romans 4:19;
Hebrews 11:11; 1 Peter 3:6

BLESSING FOCUS
Married Couples Trying to Conceive

FAITH

SCRIPTURE
"… he leadeth me …"

—Psalm 23:2b

BLESSED WOMAN FOR TODAY
SHUNAMMITE WOMAN

s a woman known for showing hospitality, I kept my house as a showpiece and always open to travelers as they passed on the outskirts of Shunem. I was kind to everyone, regardless of race, color, class, position, or title. A woman of political clout and monetary means, I was called great in social standing, faith, wisdom, and discernment. I walked and talked with kings and prophets while keeping a keen ear inclined to God's Word.

After being barren for many years, I conceived and delivered a son. When he was twelve years of age, he complained of a headache. I took him in my arms, held him from morning till noon, and watched him die in my arms. I was devastated. He was my only son, and I had waited a long time to conceive him. Even though I was consumed by grief, I stayed open to hearing God's will. In time, He showed me that, as long as I stayed faithful to His guidance, He would restore life to my son. Without a shadow of doubt, I believed God. He was true to His promise and performed a miracle before my very eyes. My son lived again.

When the prophet Elisha revived my son, he sneezed, opened his eyes, smiled, and reached for me. As I pressed his warm body against my breast, I knew that by practicing faith as God showed me, I could find serenity in every severity. My unwavering faith, unending endurance, and fervent focus on God's will led me through every test and trial to live victoriously. Three words continually spurred me on: "It is well." Many blessings flowed.

Yes, it is well. And, it is well with you and all of God's blessed women. No matter what the situation or circumstance looks like, Jesus is the reality that leads you and guides you to your greatness. He assures you that greater is He who is working within you than the happenings on the outside—personal tests, trials, and challenges. Follow His lead, and you will find miracles revealed, losses restored, and victories won. Each victory will teach you not to use woe as your answer. Instead, you will ardently affirm, "It is well" (from 2 Kings 4:26). Yes, blessed woman, it is well with your soul.

PRAYER

Heavenly Father, my Teacher and Guide, as You lead me along flat roads running straight, roads continuously twisting and bending, and others running downhill and uphill, keep me upbeat and focused on Your Word. Keep my faith holding fast to Your unfailing promises. Also, Lord, teach me how to let go and allow You to work in every area of my life. As I trust You to show me Your wisdom, I relax in peace. All is well. Thank You, Lord. Amen.

EXTENDED SCRIPTURES
2 Kings 4:8–37, 8:1–6

BLESSING FOCUS
Hospitable Women

FAITH

SCRIPTURE
"... beside the still waters."

—Psalm 23:2b

BLESSED WOMAN FOR TODAY
MARY, THE MOTHER OF JOHN MARK

*G*od blessed me with a few parcels of real estate property—not customary for Old Testament women. In one of my houses, the lavish one that was spacious and conveniently located to early Christians, I established a center of Christian worship. The most significant aspect of this ministry was a prayer group that met in the upper rooms of my house to pray for all souls at all hours of the day and night.

The spirit of God filled these rooms, and Christians in dire need found my upper rooms to be places of refuge and peace. As they poured out prayers from the depths of their souls, God heard and answered them. The full manifestation of healing miracles, Jesus' last supper, His appearances to His followers, and the infilling of His Spirit at Pentecost were either prophesied or witnessed at my house—the "mother of all churches."

Prayer is one of our best spiritual weapons. Women who do not pray leave themselves defenseless against disappointment, discouragement, and the depths of despair. Prayer invokes the human spirit to constantly communicate with the Holy Spirit. This living, loving Spirit continually fends for all women and makes intercession in every need.

When we pray, we can talk to Jesus as a best friend. We can tell Him everything—the good, not so good, embarrassing, shameful, and sinful. He hears us, shows us His compassion, forgives us, and blesses us. He wants us to lean on Him as on a bosom and rest in peace, knowing we are safe. In Him, we are protected from the turbulent waters of terrorism, worldly affairs, and outer concerns.

PRAYER

Dear Lord, my Refuge, Intercessor for my soul, and Prince of Peace, continue to lead me to the quiet places in my spirit where I can commune with Your Spirit. As You speak to me, teach me to follow You without hesitation. Show me my true unlimited potential according to Your will. Amen.

EXTENDED SCRIPTURES
Mark 14:13–16; Acts 1:12–14, 12:12–13

BLESSING FOCUS
Praying Mothers

PART TWO
BLESSING OTHERS

ften when we think we have suffered a loss, we have actually experienced a gain. We may lose material gains and later find joy in life's simple pleasures. We lose our health to heal and restore our soul. Or in the death of a loved one, we discover that the soul lives on. To lose is to gain.

Experiencing these rich awakenings helps us to receive our blessings and bless others. This keeps us in the service of the Lord. Let us praise God and see His blessings flow through open channels to us.

BLESSING OTHERS

SCRIPTURE
"He restoreth my soul ..."

—Psalm 23:3a

BLESSED WOMAN FOR TODAY
RUTH

*W*hen my mother-in-law, Naomi, was widowed in my
hometown of Moab, she decided to return alone to her home in
Bethlehem. I would hear of no such thing. Being strong-willed and
feeling bitter, she chided me. Promising to stick by her side
throughout her life, I convinced her to accept my binding words,
companionship, and comfort. Together, we set out for Bethlehem.

As two fatigued and desolate women, we—she a Hebrew citizen
and I a foreigner from Moab—reached Bethlehem. All we had was
each other. To support us, I performed the lowliest work, gleaning
ears of corn and barley in the rugged fields. Working in sunstroke
heat from daybreak to sunset kept food on our table and clothes on
our backs—both of meager means.

Over time, my hard and smart work, foresight, and resolve
helped me overcome my alien background, which was hated by
early Israel. I turned their harsh criticism into enhanced charisma
as I persevered. I won friends and influenced the land proprietors.
They saw me as responsible, empathetic, and unselfish.

Recognizing my meekness, modesty, and concern for others,
Boaz (Hebrew for "strength"), one of the rich land proprietors,
offered me respect and protection in the workplace. Molestation
was common in those hot, dusty fields. This kind and gentle "man
of most women's dreams" asked me to marry him. The birth of our
son, Obed, sprang a lineage to Jesus Christ. Through my grandson
Jesse and King David, I am the great-grandmother of Jesus.

Untiring love, faithfulness, and generosity of the soul work miracles. They build up and restore lives. They break barriers—race, class, and gender—to raise all to higher standards of living. Our lives are not our own. We are all connected, crossing continents, color lines, and creeds, giving to others, even when we see no monetary return. When we get out of our comfort zones and into covenant relationships, we grow from "What's in it for me?" to "What's in it for others?" and "How can I bless others today?" As such, we are blessed, and we will bless the whole human race.

PRAYER

Dear gracious, giving God, my Exemplar of unconditional love, thank You for giving new life to the world through Your only begotten Son. Help me to be a blessing to others today, expecting nothing in return for myself. Amen.

EXTENDED SCRIPTURES
Ruth 1:4, 2–5, 8, 14, 16, 21–22; Matthew 1:5;
John 15:12–17; 1 John 3:16–17, 26:52–54; Mark 14:36

BLESSING FOCUS
Women Who Give Untiringly and Unselfishly to Humankind

PART THREE
COMFORT

hen we take shortcuts, we can make mistakes that cost us in time, money, and relationships with others. When we compromise our health by taking the easy way out, we can experience sickness, suffering, and sorrow.

What a relief it is to know that God helps us to make sound decisions and take appropriate action in the daily affairs of our lives. Sometimes God's way takes longer than ours, but waiting on the Lord gives us an assurance of a sound solution. This assures us with peace of mind, harmony, and joy. As we enjoy these rewards from Him who gave His complete love for all—with no shortcuts— we find comfort.

COMFORT

SCRIPTURE
"... he leadeth me in the paths of righteousness ..."
—Psalm 23:3b

BLESSED WOMAN FOR TODAY
LYDIA

When God opened my heart to repentance, I accepted Him, becoming the first Christian convert in Europe. This was a crowning event in my life, because I was a successful businesswoman in the lucrative purple-dye trade.

After I was converted and baptized, my whole household was also. I had no thoughts of how I, a Christian, would appear to other business leaders, my customers, or the dyers' guild. I was not ashamed of the gospel. And, I was not worried or concerned about being rejected. Placing Christ first in my life, I changed my priorities from motivations in the secular world to things pertaining to Christ. I became a direct witness that, through faith in Christ, a businessperson can openly seek truth and still be successful in a trade or chosen field.

I converted my home into a ministry for witnessing, praying, and teaching about discipleship. I grew in my faith and fellowship to spread the good news of Jesus Christ throughout Europe and countries farther to the west.

No matter what our profession, job, trade, or business, let us never be ashamed of the good news of Jesus Christ, declaring His unconditional love and His gift of salvation. He was not and is not ashamed of us. He comes to save us, bless us, and heal us from affliction and infirmity. His way is good and leads us to avoid wrong and do what's right. This includes right attitudes, right speech, right conduct, and right living. This is not to be misunderstood as "self-righteousness." To do so would mean merely justifying our shortcomings to stay the same and not change for betterment.

COMFORT

PRAYER

Loving God, my only true Righteous One, thank You for the joy in holy living. Help me meditate on godly thoughts and speak Your words. Teach me to stay true to the desires that are acceptable in Your sight. Amen.

EXTENDED SCRIPTURES
Acts 16:13–15, 40

BLESSING FOCUS

Christian Businesswomen

Comfort

Scripture

*"… he leadeth me in the paths of righteousness
for his name's sake."*

—Psalm 23:3b

Blessed Woman for Today
Dorcas

y name, Dorcas, was a good name. Known as a
Christian woman *"full of good works"* (Acts 9:36), I was looked
upon as compassionate, devout, and benevolent. As I perched in my
upper-room window, high above the city of Joppa, I watched and
took notes about needy young people, older people in destitute
situations, widows, the fatherless, and the homeless. I felt deep
compassion for them and helped them in every way I could.
Patterned after my charity to the needy, the Dorcas Sewing
Societies sprang up worldwide.

After helping to uplift the hearts and spirits of souls in Joppa, I
became lifted up, raised from death to life. Just as the name of Jesus
brought me back to life, He continued to lift Joppa's underprivileged
people from filth, starvation, and poverty to blessed living, peace,
and prosperity.

What's in a name? A lot. We learn to trust in a good name, whether by manufacturer's brand or by person. For example, what do you think of when you hear *Good Housekeeping*, Chanel, or Jesus Christ? Most think of the highest standards of excellence. Along with the name comes character. We feel confident and find comfort when we can trust in one's name and impeccable character.

Every day we face a questionable or urgent situation that calls for demonstration of our character. We might be tempted to lie, steal, cheat, or hold back others' blessings. Just as Dorcas did, let us show our true nature intended by God—a good character, showing integrity, compassion, right thinking, and right actions in all situations.

PRAYER
Dear Righteous Redeemer, thank You for Your good character that saved me from sin and sorrow. Help me to bring my desires, character, and concern for others in harmony with God's will. Amen.

EXTENDED SCRIPTURES
Acts 9:36, 39, 40; 1 Timothy 2:9–10; Proverbs 31:13, 20

BLESSING FOCUS
*Women Living in Destitute Situations
(homeless, fatherless, motherless, abandoned)*

PART FOUR
COURAGE

ertain symbols remind us that all is well. These symbols could be an angel, a gentle stream, an orange sunrise, Calvary's cross, a cup of hot tea, a picture of Jesus, a Bible, or even chocolates. As we hold the pictures in our mind's eye, they can represent comfort, safety, and peacefulness in trying times.

The sight of the shepherd's rod and staff comforts the sheep. They vividly recall how their committed caretaker uses the rod to kill coyotes, cougars, and other wild beasts. And they relax as the shepherd uses his staff to skillfully pull a sheep from the edge of a cliff. As they dwell upon these reassuring symbols of safety and protection, sheep stay calm and confident.

COURAGE

SCRIPTURE
"Yea ..."

—Psalm 23:4a

BLESSED WOMAN FOR TODAY
LEAH

T was not as beautiful or shapely as my sister, Rachel; however, I was more spiritually minded and pious. I needed those blessed virtues in view of my father's dirty tricks to consummate a deal, giving me away in marriage in place of Rachel. My husband Jacob really loved Rachel and wanted to marry her. But, because of my father's deal, he could not have her. Instead he was stuck with me, and even though he did not love me as much as he did Rachel, I bore him his six sons and a daughter.

During this trying time of being married and knowing that my husband really longed for and loved my younger, more beautiful, petulant sister, I neither complained nor showed envy. I drew closer to God for tenderness and strength to endure. He lovingly taught me how to show courage in the midst of deceit and my husband's unfaithfulness. In my intimate relationship with God, I held tight to His comforting lifeline in the midst of deep personal grief.

By saying yes to God's will and seeking Him all the more, He blessed me with abundance, a spirit of praise, and a heart of contentment. From my son Judah sprang the line of Boaz, Jesse, David, and Jesus. And for my son Levi, God showed His favor in the priesthood.

Although we might not always agree with an unfair or unbearable situation, God will reveal His will when we cry out to Him and pray. Often pressing tests such as a "bad" marriage, an unfaithful husband, a "bad" boss, broken promises, troublesome teenagers, a dead-end job, or deadbeat dads must be worked out for a greater future gain. God's plan and timetable are often a lot different from ours. All the more, we can seek Him for guidance, purpose, direction, and hope. We must faithfully endure. Then He will hear our prayers and answer them.

PRAYER

Dear Everlasting Father and Lover of our souls, help me to say yes to Your presence and power. As I abide in You night and day, You promised to never leave me nor forsake me. Your promise anchors me. Help me to look to You for everlasting love and complete satisfaction in all areas of my life. Amen.

EXTENDED SCRIPTURES
Genesis 29:30–35, 40:31; Ruth 4:11; Luke 3:23, 31–33

BLESSING FOCUS
Women Who Feel Unloved by the Men They Love
(father, brother, husband, son)

COURAGE

COURAGE

SCRIPTURE
"... though I walk through the valley of the shadow of death ..."
—Psalm 23:4a

BLESSED WOMAN FOR TODAY
DINAH

I was the youngest and only daughter of my mother, Leah, and father, Jacob. I pray that the immorality and brutality that victimized me as a teenager did not stem from the long-suffering and many struggles my mother endured, as my father withheld his love from her.

It was as though I popped out of my mother's womb, was written off, and soon forgotten. I was not one of the sons of my father Jacob, so he did not name one of the tribes in my name as he did for my brothers. After I was brutally raped—in the name of love—my father did nothing to bring justice to Shechem, my rapist. My brothers were the ones who brought bloody vengeance against him, saying he treated me, an innocent, virgin teenager, worse than a prostitute. What a contrast for one living in royalty!

Blessed women, although we cannot always prevent rape within our sisterhood, let us not ignore this evil, abusive act by men. Let us not turn away in silence while rape victims scream within and without. Let us act as our sisters' keepers and as wise advocates for rescue workers who remove them from their places of violation and take them to their secret, safe havens.

We must be quick to comfort rape victims and show them services and resources to help heal their deep wounds. Let us help restore their dignity and campaign for stiff penalties for the egregious acts of these ungodly misguided perpetrators. Let's ask God to help all women see that He always works on our behalf, even in our pain, shame, discomfort, and discouragement. He will show us how He works within our disappointment to help us find His appointment for our blessed lives.

PRAYER

Omnipotent God of mercy and grace, help me to believe in Your power working throughout every situation, bad and good. Help me to call upon You quickly. Heal my wounds and restore me. Show me how to find Your peace, comfort, joy, and redeeming love. Thank You for sticking closer than any other. Amen.

EXTENDED SCRIPTURES
Genesis 30:21, 34:1–34, 46:15; 2 Samuel 13:1–22; Psalm 31

BLESSING FOCUS
Rape Victims

COURAGE

Courage

Scripture
"… I will fear no evil …"

—Psalm 23:4b

Blessed Woman for Today
Nameless Women

We were the daughters, sisters, singles, wives, *married mothers, widows, unwed mothers, ministers, single heads of households, the celibate, and other unnamed women in the Bible. Although nameless, we touched human lives and helped to shape futures. We gave hope and encouragement. We imparted wisdom. We challenged people's faith, witnessed to nonbelievers, destroyed pagan worship, and sacrificed our lives for the sake of the gospel of Jesus Christ.*

Many of us set personal standards. For example, when married, some of us did not take our husbands' names (e.g., daughters of Zelophehad). Others showed courage when our fathers sold us as slaves and gave us to be married, to birth sons who would perpetuate the family line.

Still others were raised from the dead, married foreigners, and wept publicly for the deceased. One of us, the Ephraim Levite's concubine, was raped repeatedly and left to die. Later, she was cut into twelve pieces and sent far distances to the twelve tribes. This was the worst crime ever committed, whether to males or females (see Judges 19:30).

Many of today's women—who will remain nameless for obvious reasons—face similar persecution, personal trials, tests, and tribulation. We face the injustices and evils of rape, incest, betrayal, murder, sexism, racism, sexual harassment, harsh criticism, incurable diseases, and physical, emotional, and financial abuse.

Through it all, women have an unending hope, knowing that Christ rewards us as we come into an intimate relationship with Him. Just as women went to Jesus at the Crucifixion, the tomb, and the Resurrection, we can go to Him at the throne of grace, where He intercedes and continually looks after women's well-being. Through faith, we as women can find strength for the persevering of our souls. We can put hope in God's care, believing that with God all things are possible as we believe in Him.

PRAYER

Dear Lord, truly, You are my sufficient provision. You are the joy of my salvation and the Savior of my life. Thank You for drawing close to me and showing me a way to escape from trouble. Help me to draw closer to You because You are the light that dispels all darkness, creates order from chaos, and rights every wrong. In You, I will fear no evil; in Jesus' name. Amen.

EXTENDED SCRIPTURES
Psalm 27, 91, 139

BLESSING FOCUS
Female Athletes and Women in the Military

COURAGE

SCRIPTURE
"... for thou art with me ..."

—Psalm 23:4c

BLESSED WOMAN FOR TODAY
SAMSON'S MOTHER

ever mind my name. I bore none in the record but was introduced as the wife of a certain Manoah of Zorah (Judges 13:2). Maybe if I had insisted on being popular, you would not have known my famous son, Samson. He was a gift from God, prophesied by an angel to be dedicated to God's service. A simple, spiritual woman who trusted in God, I believed the angel and reared Samson to refrain from any intoxicating drink and taking razors to his raven locks of hair. God had placed a sacred calling upon him.

As Samson grew to manhood, I prayed as never before. Although unmatched in his physical strength, his greatest weakness was women. I objected to every one of them—prostitutes and seductresses—as my son played to their lusts, lures, and intrigue. Every time he succumbed completely. He fell the hardest from the enticements of evil Delilah. For 1,100 pieces of silver from each of several Philistine lords, she betrayed Samson and caused him to lose his strength. After regaining it, he stood between two pillars supporting a great assembly hall in Philistia, grabbed them between his muscular arms, and pulled them down. When the building collapsed, he perished underneath, along with hundreds of its occupants. Some Israelites called this a heroic suicide because in so doing, Samson destroyed the oppressors of his people.

We want the best for our loved ones, and when we see them behaving out of God's will, we ache for them. When they naively fall into deadly traps such as unleashed lust, materialism, drugs, greed, and crime, we call upon God to be with them and work it out for good. No matter how much we counsel, coach, console, or scold, often they continue to follow what proves only to weaken or destroy them.

This is the time for us to cast all our cares on Him who hears our prayers. He sees all and knows all. Instead of trying to "fix" them or understand why they keep repeating the same costly mistakes, God wants us to spend our energy and time trusting in Him and learning about His peace that passes all understanding. As we surrender to God, He comforts our souls. He whispers He will never leave us or abandon us when we sin or make a mistake. Further, He assures us with "Be still and know that I AM God" (Psalm 46:10).

COURAGE

PRAYER

Dear Comforter, Redeemer, and Prince of Peace, You are all-knowing and everywhere-present. Help me to repent when I sin. Keep me faithful to You. As the Holy Spirit guides me, help me to be useful to You, according to Your will, Your way, and Your perfect timing. Amen.

EXTENDED SCRIPTURES
Judges 13:2, 11, 19–23; Judges 14:5;
Judges 16:4, 6, 10, 12–13, 18; Hebrews 11:32

BLESSING FOCUS
Suicide Survivors

COURAGE

SCRIPTURE
"... thy rod and thy staff ..."

—Psalm 23:4d

BLESSED WOMAN FOR TODAY
ZIPPORAH

knew a lot about sheep. Often I tended the flock of my priestly father, Jethro. I met my husband, Moses, as my seven sisters and I tended my father's flock in the lowlands. He helped us find water for our sheep.

I had often observed caring shepherds as they threw their rods across great distances. These custom-made extensions of the shepherds' powerful arms would attack their intended targets with astonishing precision. When I herded sheep, I used my rod to guide sheep or prod them along the trail. Sometimes I would discipline and correct the wayward ones. Sheep knew that my rod carried a sense of power, authority, discipline, and defense against danger.

On the other hand, my staff was a symbol for concern, care, and comfort. While I leaned against my staff, I felt at ease, comfortable, and peaceful, knowing all was safe and well for my sheep. If I saw a lamb about to fall off a cliff or hanging from a tree branch on the side of an incline, I would extend my staff to firmly catch hold of it and bring it to safety. As the other sheep watched, they felt safe and comforted.

Jesus, the Good Shepherd, uses His power, dominion, and authority to fend for us, protect us, and bring us to safety with His rod and staff. At times, He uses His rod as His Word to gently nudge us. This reminds us that "we are touching and agreeing" on His will (1 Samuel 20:23; Matthew 18:19). He uses His staff as the Holy Spirit to help us keep the mind of Christ. This is His confirmation that He is with us, and we abide in Him.

However, when we see ourselves as shy, weak, fearful, "not good enough," or feeling unsure of ourselves, we can picture God's rod and staff in our minds. This will help assure us that we are confident and sure-footed as we take on responsibilities. His gentle prompting reminds us to follow His will. His gentle touch helps us feel safe and secure when we get into jams and scrapes or escape near misses.

PRAYER

Good Shepherd, thank You for Your presence, wisdom, power, and intelligence working to remind me that You are with me, and all is well. Lead me through Your Word and teach me. Let Your Spirit work to bring my desires in harmony with Your will. Amen.

EXTENDED SCRIPTURES
Exodus 2:21, 4:20–26, 18:2–3

BLESSING FOCUS
Mismatched Marriages

COURAGE

SCRIPTURE
"… they comfort me."

—Psalm 23:4d

BLESSED WOMAN FOR TODAY
ASENATH

*had a lot for which to be thankful: my husband,
Joseph; a good marriage; and my two sons, Manasseh and
Ephraim. However, I am most thankful that God showed me how to
stop worshiping my sun-gods, repent, and turn to Him.*

*As I grew to know the only true God—Jehovah—I relied on
Him with all my heart and soul. God blessed my family and me by
my devotion to Him.*

There comes a time in our lives when the Good Shepherd will remind us to turn our attention to Him. Then we can search ourselves to find ways to change. At other times, He will pull us out of dilemmas and back to His will. Whether guided along the way or pulled to the fold, we can rest in the satisfaction that the Comforter comes tenderly and compassionately to show us how to make the right decisions. Using spiritual discernment, we can decide according to God's will and act with confidence. We can enjoy harmony and peaceful outcomes.

PRAYER

Thank You, Good Shepherd, for drawing near to me and me near to You. Rescue me from what is not pleasing in Your sight. Tend to my needs with compassion and unconditional love. Help me to stay on the path You have prepared for me. As You lead me, help me to follow You. Amen.

EXTENDED SCRIPTURES
Genesis 41:45, 50, 46:20; Acts 7:22

BLESSING FOCUS
New Believers

COURAGE

SCRIPTURE
"… thou art with me; thy rod and thy staff they comfort me."
—Psalm 23:4c,d

BLESSED WOMAN FOR TODAY
ESTHER

*W*hen I was left fatherless, cousin Mordecai adopted me and relocated me to a Persian court ruled by King Ahasuerus. Attracted by my striking beauty and intelligence, the Persian king married me and crowned me queen. My husband did not know he had married a foreigner—a Jewess among other Jewish captives taken to Persia.

When I learned of a plot to slaughter all local Jews and seize their property, I was ready to reveal my Jewish identity. I knew that I would risk giving up my regal robes and royal crown. As I trusted in God, I appealed to my husband to cancel the massacre decree. Although he could not, due to Persian law, he did authorize cousin Mordecai to send out another decree, giving Jews the right to carry arms in self-defense.

My people slew their Persian enemies and paved the way for our nation. This was because I trusted more in doing what was right than what was convenient for my comfort and materialistic indulgence. Today, Jews continue to celebrate Purim Festival in my honor on March 14 and 15 each year.

God's Word is our priceless possession. It helps us discern right from wrong. It can trouble our minds until we revert from lie to truth and from cheating to honesty. It will help uncover hidden things to make the truth in a situation plain. God's Spirit humbles us to surrender to His will. Then we let go of pride, arrogance, and high-mindedness. We act with authenticity and integrity.

Through His providential care, God equips us with decisiveness and charm to apply where needed. We behave honorably and peaceably in our daily duties and relationships with others.

PRAYER

Gracious Holy Spirit, our Comforter and Friend, lead me away from pretense and arrogance. Guide me by Your grace and mercy so that I will show tenderness, compassion, and genuine concern as I serve loved ones and others. Amen.

EXTENDED SCRIPTURES
Book of Esther, Psalm 139:23–24;
Proverbs 13:22; John 16:13

BLESSING FOCUS
*Orphaned Children
(by greed, pride, selfishness, war, and disease)*

COURAGE

PART FIVE
KEEPING PROMISES

s it easier for you to make promises or to accept them from others? We can trust people who keep their promises. And, we feel trustworthy when we keep ours.

Jesus promises to go ahead of us before any kind of change in our lives—personal and professional. He acts strategically, decisively, and timely to thoroughly prepare the way for our good.

As we face any kind of concern, we can trust in His definite way and His true Word, because He promises that His Word will not return to Him void, or without a good result. But, it shall accomplish that which He pleases. And, His Word always prospers in those things wherever He sends it (translated from Isaiah 55:11).

Jesus keeps His promises. He watches over His words, and we can rest in knowing that He always watches over us.

KEEPING PROMISES

SCRIPTURE
"Thou preparest …"

—Psalm 23:5a

BLESSED WOMAN FOR TODAY
MARTHA OF BETHANY

n the new millennium, I would have been called Martha Stewart Jr. As a perfectionist and impeccable hostess, entertaining was my gift and passion. I was known for zealously attending to the minutest details of culinary delight and etiquette, and the townspeople entrusted notable feasts and banquets to me. I devoted myself to perfect preparation, checking my list at least three times. I gave my guests nothing less than the best in correct social conventions. I practiced proper protocol for welcoming guests, table settings, seating at the tables, and table manners. My food presentations looked like works of fine art. It was not customary for women to have such freedom in preparing lavish meals, entertaining, and serving as hostesses.

Our caretaker and provider, Jesus, prepares perfectly for us—mastering the minutest detail of our needs. In fact, because He is providential, He knows what we need before we ask Him. Before His death, burial, and resurrection, He prepared a perfect place so that where He is, we can be there with Him (John 14:3). When He ascended into Heaven, He sat down at the right of the throne of grace to mediate and make intercession for our prayers and special requests. Jesus' perfect preparation provides us sufficient spiritual feeding, comfort, and peace.

PRAYER

Thank You, Lord, for keeping Your promises and taking care of all my needs. Help me to value the labor of Your perfect preparation and to trust You to keep me comforted, safe, and secure. Amen.

EXTENDED SCRIPTURES
Luke 10:38–42;
John 11:1–12:23, 19–21, 24, 30, 39, 12:1–2, 14:2–3

BLESSING FOCUS
Hospitality Workers

KEEPING PROMISES

SCRIPTURE

"… a table before me in the presence of mine enemies …"

—Psalm 23:5a

BLESSED WOMAN FOR TODAY
ABIGAIL

*W*hen I heard that my house and household were
about to be attacked by almost six hundred angry men, I thought
quickly and lost no time. My household helpers and I prepared
hundreds of pounds of delicate fruit, raisin and fig cakes, and the
best-prepared bread. My field hands lined up donkeys and loaded
them to capacity with the fine food delicacies, animal skins, roasted
grain, and other fine gifts. My husband was too intoxicated to help,
so my household helpers, field hands, and I rode the donkeys over
rough roads and through ravines to reach the assailants.

When I met the mob, I interceded for my household with fine
food and gracious conversation. Through faith in God, I addressed
them with decisiveness and dignity. My speech has been heralded as
the longest one recorded in the Bible. It caused the mob to retreat,
and I saved my household from death and destruction.

Jesus Christ, our Good Shepherd, suffered deep injury, sorrow, and pain to save His household, His sons and daughters. He experienced deep pain and disappointment firsthand and today He can relate to our desires, temptations, weaknesses, and other critical needs. He understands what our lives are like and assures us: There is no temptation or pain known to us that is not common to man, and God will always give us a way to escape (from 1 Corinthians 10:13).

To soothe our worries, He rounds up the finest and most abundant supply of food and drink, attractively arranges it on a well-appointed banquet table, and beckons, "Come and dine. You can feast at my sumptuous table any time." He continues: "The meat represents My mighty strength and power; the bread, My daily substance; the fowl, the unending freedom I have given you; the various fruits, My rich rewards; the vegetables, My untiring energy; and the water, My everlasting life."

When we eat fully and drink freely, we never hunger or thirst. We are filled with the Spirit. Knowing that we are Spirit-fed and fully equipped for battle, our enemies quickly retreat, and we are safe.

PRAYER

Constant companion, most gracious Host and Provider, help me to come to Your table with thanksgiving for Your love and constant care. Through Your Spirit, help me to stay reassured of Your close, cordial presence. Help me to be quick to praise You and honor You. Amen.

EXTENDED SCRIPTURES
1 Samuel 25:1–44, 27:3, 30:5;
2 Samuel 2:2, 3:3; 1 Chronicles 3:1

BLESSING FOCUS
Wives Making the Best of a Difficult Marriage

KEEPING PROMISES

SCRIPTURE
*"Thou preparest a table before me in the presence
of mine enemies …"*

—Psalm 23:5a

BLESSED WOMAN FOR TODAY
MARY OF BETHANY

*M*y sister, Martha, delighted herself in serving
household guests with the finest display of generous hospitality. Her
heart felt especially happy when Jesus visited our home and ate from
her dinner table. My deep passion kept me zealous in a different
direction—inward. As I sat at Jesus' feet and listened to His
teaching, my heart felt nurtured, nourished, and blessed.

As I learned the true meaning of "table," I felt safe and
protected. A table is not only for displaying delicious food. An
African word for table is "mesa," a high, flat-topped plateau, such
as the world-renowned Table Mountain near Cape Town, South
Africa, or an American mesa in Arizona. The attentive shepherd
spends many hours risking his life to prepare the high mesa for the
sheep to spend the summer. As he goes ahead of the sheep, he
surveys the wild, rough terrain. He prepares the high tableland "in
the presence of enemies." He makes it safe by removing thorny
bushes and killing ferocious coyotes, cougars, and other predators.
He clears branches and dead leaves from streams, and dams up
fresh water supply. The aggressive yet kind shepherd does all that is
humanly possible to make the table in the highlands safe, secure,
and nourishing. He prepares it for the sheep to graze peacefully
and free of worry.

Blessed women, Jesus our attentive Shepherd keeps looking out for our welfare. He went ahead of us to suffer every possible pain of ridicule and "woundedness" to know our grief, struggles, and sorrow. Today, He continues to go ahead of every circumstance we could possibly encounter because our extremity is His opportunity to prepare a table of care, compassion, and comfort.

He goes ahead of us to make every possible provision for our new jobs, challenging assignments, marriages, families, doctors' diagnoses, hospital stays, vacations, pregnancies, new bosses, coworkers, new homes, performance reviews, and pay reviews. We can relax and rest in the confidence of His selflessness and eagle-eye care. He thoroughly prepares the table before us "for His good name's sake." We can trust Him.

PRAYER
Dear Lord, all-powerful, providential Shepherd and Keeper of my soul, thank You for the peace I find in my intimate companionship with You. Forgive me when I do not fully understand Your perfect preparation. Help me to relax in the reality of Your perfect care. Amen.

EXTENDED SCRIPTURES
Luke 10:38–42; John 11:1–39, 12:2–11; Mark 14:3–9

BLESSING FOCUS
Women Who Believe They Are "Not Good Enough"

KEEPING PROMISES

PART SIX
DELIVERANCE

h, how sweet it is when someone lovingly places a Band-Aid on our cut finger or toe. When they add a sweet kiss or comforting hugs, we forget the pain and we feel loved and assured of a speedy healing.

Jesus knows every hurt, pain, and pressure that we feel. He gently spreads bountiful balms of His compassion to every wound. As He pours out His Spirit of love and life, He delivers us. He heals us, and we feel highly favored and blessed beyond measure.

DELIVERANCE

SCRIPTURE

"... thou anointest my head with oil ..."

—Psalm 23:5b

BLESSED WOMAN FOR TODAY
MARY MAGDALENE

*M*y heart, mind, and soul were dedicated to Christ. I loved Him and committed my life to Him. Following Him from place to place, I ministered to Him and lived to serve Him with my best spiritual gifts. I was completely satisfied with my allegiance to the truth of His being. However, I had not always been so totally committed to Christ.

You see, when I was younger, I was possessed with seven demons. These rendered me mentally and emotionally diseased and spiritually depraved. Depressed and downcast, I suffered from constant fear and low self-esteem. Wallowing in self-pity caused me to feel bitter and suicidal.

My interactions with others were always a disaster. Often I showed discord, jealously, resentment, and anger. A cloud of "I'm not good enough" always hung over my head, making me feel that I had to defend myself or argue with people. Eventually, I turned to idolatry, the lowest form of pagan worship. While in the depths of my despair, I found Jesus.

Loving me and working as the Great Physician, He cast out the seven demons, delivered me, and took me to the height of ecstasy— joy and peace in Him. He taught me how to love myself and harmonize with others. I had never felt so free, whole, and complete as I did through His fresh anointing! This true transformation healed me completely, and I continually enjoyed an intimate relationship with Jesus. My joy was complete.

A wounded woman who transforms to the truth of her being—happy, healthy, whole, complete, and free—finds the golden key to complete soul satisfaction. Today, Jesus promises to heal all wounds, whatever the cause—child molestation, domestic violence, deep disappointment, abandonment, miscarriage, rejection, suicide attempts, sexual harassment, unresolved anger, racism, sexism, discrimination, abortion, or loss of a loved one. Cast all your cares on Him. Give every concern to Him, because He cares for you (1 Peter 5:7). And He promises to restore your health as He heals your wounds (see Jeremiah 30:17). Trust in Him, and He will deliver you.

PRAYER

Holy Redeemer and Transformer of my life, help me to rely on You completely to care for my needs. With Your mercy and love, lift me from the tombs of despair to the reality of Your healing power. I will follow You and exalt Your name forever. Amen.

EXTENDED SCRIPTURES
Matthew 27:56, 61, 28:1; Mark 15:40, 47, 16:9;
Luke 8:2, 24:10; John 19:25, 20:1, 11, 16, 18;
Proverbs 3:8–9; Psalm 91; Isaiah 55:11

BLESSING FOCUS
Women Struggling to Break Evil Strongholds

DELIVERANCE

DELIVERANCE

"... my cup ..."

—Psalm 23:5c

BLESSED WOMAN FOR TODAY
DAMARIS

I was proud of my great intellect, reasoning ability, and analytical skills. This was, until I accepted the teachings of the Apostle Paul. I learned to integrate thinking abilities with the receptivity of my soul to be guided by intuition, affections, emotions, and spiritual discernment.

As I was delivered from my "headiness," my awareness of my personal ego decreased. I turned my attention to the marvelous infillment of the Holy Spirit. I began to experience peace, comfort, and joy as never before.

Our "cup" represents a happy experience, good fortune, consolation, or blessings. Beyond the satisfaction of God's presence in the here and now, our cup is the blessing of eternal life that is given without regard to whether we are rich or poor or female or male.

All too often, we go along in our daily affairs, taking pride in how we have "made it"—we made it on our own or we are self-made. Like Damaris, we can allow our thinking abilities to take first place ahead of the leading and guiding of the Holy Spirit. This can happen when we make a snap decision: when we act without praying first to make a major purchase, take the job of our dreams, get involved in a serious relationship, or accept a marriage proposal. Consulting with God first leads to right actions. Also, this helps us find peace. All good things find their way into our circumstances when we believe God and trust His goodness.

PRAYER

My Redeemer and Counselor, help me to seek You first in all things pertaining to my life and my loved ones. Teach me to always see that Your will for me is good all the time. Amen.

EXTENDED SCRIPTURES
Acts 17:34; John 18:11

BLESSING FOCUS
Women in Technology

DELIVERANCE

DELIVERANCE

SCRIPTURE
"... my cup runneth over."

—Psalm 23:5c

BLESSED WOMAN FOR TODAY
THE UNTOUCHABLE WOMAN

I had suffered from an incurable disease for more than twelve years. Because it involved nonstop bleeding and I was a woman, I was considered unclean, an outcast, and untouchable. As though that were not enough to get me down, I was also broke. I had spent all my money—what little I had—on many doctors. None could heal me.

However, I knew that rejection, discouragement, and disappointment were not His appointment for me. Because He was the Great Physician promised by Malachi, I had to find Jesus soon. I knew that if I could just touch the fringes of His long robe, I would be healed.

Then it happened! I found Him! I heard His footsteps! I saw His compassionate face! Although the crowds tried to restrict contact with Him, I, this unclean thing, pressed through and touched Him. Through faith in Him, I was healed instantly! Unlike the bigoted men in the crowd, Jesus acknowledged me and spoke to me eye-to-eye. His words confirmed that I had been healed and made whole. As He validated me, I was delivered from my invalid condition.

I was healed and saved. My cup overflowed.

Whatever personal challenge, sickness, incurable disease, or physical, mental, emotional, or financial condition we face today, we must believe that there is nothing too hard for God. Nothing and "no thing." He knows firsthand every human condition and is able to heal us.

However, when our loved ones (or we) are not healed in the physical body, we can find comfort in knowing they (and we) remain in His presence and are whole spiritually. This is because to be absent from the body is to be present with God (2 Corinthians 5:8). After we die, our physical bodies decay. The soul and spirit live on in the eternal realm. We can keep the hope that our souls will meet the souls of our loved ones, and we will live forever.

PRAYER

Overcomer and Advocate, thank You for perfect healing in mind, body, spirit, and soul through Your Son. Help me to accept Your will, which is never "the less," but "all the more"; in Jesus' name. Amen.

EXTENDED SCRIPTURES
Mark 5:25–34; Leviticus 15:25–33; Luke 8:43–48; Psalm 34

BLESSING FOCUS
Hospice Workers and Their Patients
(cancer patients and others suffering from incurable diseases)

DELIVERANCE

PART SEVEN
VICTORY

What words can you speak with certainty? "I love you." "I will never leave you." "I am your bosom friend." "You can depend on me," or "I'm here for you."

Jesus meant it when He said that He came to give us abundant life in Him and privilege to use it freely. He does not lie or withhold His good. We live victoriously when we accept God's goodness.

Victorious living in Jesus never ends. It lives on forever as our heritage and legacy. When we live victoriously, we express the truth of our being, daughters of Jesus Christ. The lyrics created from victorious living make up our songs of praise and joy.

After successfully leading ten thousand troops in battle, Deborah, a prophetess, judge, and warrior, brought her country to "rest" for forty years. As she triumphed, she sang her victory song to her people. She cried out with gusto and delight, "March on, my soul, with might!" (Judges 5:2–7, 20, 21). Her legacy lives today.

God bestows victorious living as our blessed assurance that wherever we go, He goes with us. He will keep us strong in battle and mighty in deliverance. God promises victorious living for us now and forever.

VICTORY

SCRIPTURE
"Surely ..."

—Psalm 23:6a

BLESSED WOMAN FOR TODAY
RIZPAH

As I watched them bury the former King Saul, his three sons, and five grandsons, I wondered whether any woman had experienced greater tragedy or endured deeper pain than I had for the past six months. I seriously doubted it.

In a fit of macho revenge, my two sons, fathered by Saul, and his five grandsons by his daughter, Merab, were hanged on a hillside, deserted, and left without a proper burial. This was against the law and a strike against this royal family.

I had stood by my family as they lived and would do so during their deaths. With no provision for ceremonial mourning or anyone to help me bury my men, I resolved to rely on God. Surely He would send someone. To wait it out, I quickly built a makeshift shelter from a weather-beaten rock and a sackcloth made from goat and camel hair. This was meager protection from hungry birds of prey by day and jackals and lions prowling to drag away my men's decomposing bodies during the night.

From mid-April to early October, I spent many sleepless nights calling on God. I asked Him to protect me and send someone to help me properly bury the corpses of my men. For countless hours I continued my prayer vigil, waited, and watched. Finally, God touched the heart of King David. When he heard about the loyalty and courage I showed throughout my bitter circumstances, he agreed to come and make proper burial. He arrived with the bones of Saul and his son Jonathan. We buried them along with the seven corpses I had watched over—long overdue for the grave. God had heard my cry. He honored my faithfulness and answered my prayer.

YOU ARE A BLESSED WOMAN

Rizpah's deep devotion to her family and unrelenting faith in God helped her endure her six-month crisis. When she lived to see her just reward, sorrow turned to joy. All women—American and those around the globe—can relate to Rizpah's critical situation and long period of suffering.

As we "watch and wait" for loved ones, we must show loyalty and long-suffering. We must pray for God to protect our children from noonday vultures and night-prowling lions seeking to destroy precious souls with drugs, alcohol, pornography, prostitution, street crimes, and other deadly devices. We hold prayer vigils for runaway teenagers, abducted babies, and missing children. We sit by the bedsides of loved ones suffering from long-term illnesses and incurable diseases. As we grieve the loss of loved ones, we wear our own sackcloth.

We pray that husbands will return chaste and undefiled to the beds of their own wives. We ask God to cause deadbeat dads and runaway husbands to assume the responsibilities placed on them by God. We pray, watch, and wait as loved ones serve prison sentences. We endure the unknown as our men and women serve in the military or fight in combat.

As women, whether urban, suburban, or rural, abide in Christ and persevere with love, peace, patience, gentleness, goodness, and faith, for surely God will deliver. He will send the right person with the right answer and right reward. Surely, God hears and delivers at the right time.

PRAYER

Defender and Deliverer, surely You show favor and stay with me as I endure circumstances beyond my control. Help me know what I can control, what I cannot, and the end result that only You can control. And although I may feel all alone, help me to see that I am "all-one" with You. Constantly remind me that in Spirit and in truth, I am never alone. Thank You, God, for always being there for me, whether it is night or day. Amen.

EXTENDED SCRIPTURES
2 Samuel 3:7, 21:8–14

BLESSING FOCUS
Women Who Wait

VICTORY

VICTORY

SCRIPTURE
"… goodness and …"

—Psalm 23:6a

BLESSED WOMAN FOR TODAY
MARY, THE MOTHER OF JESUS

ow is it that a simple, everyday, teenage peasant girl could be so richly blessed, honored, and revered among millions of women? I had never worn fine clothes or expensive jewelry. Never stepped foot in an ornate palace or even ventured too far past Palestine. Yet God chose me to fulfill His promised peace, goodness, and joy to the world.

Calling me to be the blessed mother of Christ was more than I could have ever thought possible. However, when the angel of the Lord told me I would be, I trusted God totally and surrendered to His will.

Blessed women who are branded as poor, social outcasts, welfare cases, or not "in the know" or "who's who" must not allow themselves to feel insignificant or burdened by humankind's weighty standards for status and self-esteem. Instead, all women must know "whose we are"—Christ's—and that we are highly favored without regard to our age, race, gender, neighborhood, job, ability, or disability. We are highly favored by God. He sees us as good for His service and glory.

Take your reward of goodness to someone and render a simple, selfless service. Your well-doing will cheer a broken heart or ignite a spark of hope in a downcast spirit. Repeating this over time, you will spread goodness, to significantly change a home, community, or country. God will notice your kindness. Your good gifts will be cherished in memories and brought to light in times of great need.

PRAYER

Heavenly Father, Lord and Savior, Redeemer of my soul, thank You for Your grace and love. Help me to always receive You with an open mind and humble spirit. Keep me trusting in Your possibilities and my God-given potentiality. Amen.

EXTENDED SCRIPTURES
Matthew 1:16–20, 2:11, 13:55; Mark 6:3;
Luke 1:27, 30, 34, 38–41, 2:5–34; Acts 1:14; John 19:25;
Psalm 31:21, 117:2; 2 Samuel 2:6; Peter 1:5–7

BLESSING FOCUS
Expectant Mothers

VICTORY

SCRIPTURE
"... mercy shall follow me all the days of my life ..."
—Psalm 23:6a

BLESSED WOMAN FOR TODAY
GOMER

*W*hen the prophet Hosea married me, he knew I was a prostitute. Several times during our marriage I was unfaithful, and each time he forgave me and took me back. He even kept me when it was questionable who the father of two of my children was.

Throughout my impurity and infidelity, he stayed steadfast in love and patience. He was never spiteful or judgmental. What more could I ask for than to love myself, forgive myself, repent, and seek God to help me turn away from adultery? I did not, however, and continued to hang out in the streets and sleep with many men.

When Jesus showed compassion and forgave the adulterous woman brought before Him, she was saved. God was ready to save Gomer, but she was unwilling to repent.

Today, we can be healed by the lessons from these two unfaithful women. God is loving and quick to forgive a woman who commits adultery. When she repents, God will show His faithfulness to her, and will forgive her. Without judgment or condemnation, He will continue to minister to her. His mercy will follow as He restores her. He will stay in close companionship with her.

Also, God forgives us when we are unfaithful in our spiritual marriage with Him. Abiding by His covenant with us, He continually shows us His mercy and delivers us.

PRAYER

Dear gracious and merciful Savior, do not leave me in my temptation. As I repent, forgive me and deliver me from my sin. Teach me to stay true to my marriage-tie with You. Help me to glorify You wherever I go. Amen.

EXTENDED SCRIPTURES
Hosea 1:1–3; Matthew 19:4–6; Deuteronomy 22:22

BLESSING FOCUS
Women Struggling with Destructive Habits and Eating Disorders

VICTORY

SCRIPTURE
"Surely goodness and mercy shall follow me
all the days of my life ..."

—Psalm 23:6a

BLESSED WOMAN FOR TODAY
DEBORAH

I was a multitalented woman before my time. The only woman in the Bible placed in public power and control during a time of political unrest, I was a judge and keeper of the tabernacle lamps (humble task for so great a woman as I). Also, people knew my sterling reputation as a poet, prophetess, ruler, and warrior. I was one who encouraged others.

As I took on such tall tasks, I kept an intimate relationship with God by hearing Him, believing Him, and acting on His promises. He chose me to lead in war and bring His people from bondage to peace. I was victorious in battle, and my land enjoyed political rest for forty years!

Twenty-first century journalists would describe Deborah as a "superwoman with x-ray vision," "fixer of trouble," "supermom," and "warrior." Christian writers would acclaim all praise, honor, and glory to God, who never failed to show Deborah the way to victory.

Today's women face spiritual warfare at home and work, in communities and neighborhoods, in the public and private sectors, in churches and synagogues, and in careers commonly held by men. Whether preparing to lead, leading in front, or following up from the rear, let us be encouraged by Deborah, whose name means "bee."

A close look at the exceptional nature of the bumblebee will show how God's power worked in Deborah. The bumblebee is a very active insect and defies all scientific laws about insect flying. Because of its size and enlarged hind feet, bumblebees are not built to take off and fly, but they do.

Women who, like Deborah, listen to God and trust Him, perform beyond human calculations or belief. They advance to valiant victory and celebrate triumphantly and publicly.

"No eye has seen, no ear has heard, and no mind has imagined what God has prepared for those who love him" (1 Corinthians 2:9, NLT). Let's walk by faith in God and not by the folly of others.

PRAYER

Lord, my Inheritance and Captain of my soul, help me to say yes to Your call. Make me arise, go forward, and follow You. Help me to possess Your spiritual leading, listen to Your wise counsel, and persevere by faith to attain victory. I will glorify Your name before the people. Amen.

EXTENDED SCRIPTURES
Judges 4–5

BLESSING FOCUS
Women in Combat

VICTORY

"... and I will dwell in the house of the Lord ..."
—Psalm 23:6b

BLESSED WOMAN FOR TODAY
MIRIAM

*F*rom the day my brother Moses led us Israelites from bondage in Pharaoh's Egypt to the wilderness outside the Promised Land, I knew I would live in many houses. I lived in tents and primitive houses called "booths." These were made from leafy boughs from some of the first forests. As we were a nomadic group of people, I ate and slept in caves and other dwelling places not made by human hands.

Formed by God, these natural houses were sometimes clouds by day, protecting us from the scorching sun or a pillar of fire by night, leading us along a path to safety. At other times, our house was a house within—peace and comfort in the indwelling Holy Spirit.

Whether living under a man-made roof or the luminous sky dome created by God, I always felt at home when I prayed. This kept me feeling the closeness of my relatedness with God.

For today's women, God's "home" is filled with unconditional love, peace, joy, and radiant life. His welcome mat reads, "Come to me, all of you who are weary and carry heavy burdens, and I will give you rest" (Matthew 11:28, NLT).

As we obey and enter into His rest, He opens His arms widely to receive us, along with our sorrows, grief, heartaches, and bellyaches. Holding us to His bosom, He tells us we have come home. Dwelling there, we feel safe and secure.

When spending time away from our home address, whether at work, school, a supermarket, a mall, on a business trip, or on a vacation, we take the "house of the Lord" with us. This is the abiding presence of the Holy Spirit that assures us that as we dwell in Him, He dwells in us. He watches over us, protects us, and keeps us close to "home."

PRAYER

Hiding Place, Protector, and Lover of my soul, thank You for allowing me to dwell in Your holy presence. Help me to stay in Your dwelling place for peace, comfort, safety, and security. As I draw closer to You, thank You for receiving me. Amen.

EXTENDED SCRIPTURES
Exodus 15:20–21; Numbers 12:1–15, 20:1, 26:59; Deuteronomy 24:4; Micah 6:4; Matthew 28:11

BLESSING FOCUS
The Homeless

VICTORY

SCRIPTURE
"... for ever."

—Psalm 23:6b

BLESSED WOMAN FOR TODAY
WOMEN WHO SAW

*W*e loved Jesus and stayed devoted to Him from His birth to death to resurrection. We ministered to Him, wept for Him in His suffering and sorrow, and triumphed with Him in His glory. We are the Marys whom Jesus knew and loved.

Mary, the mother of Jesus, delivered Him into the world, nurtured Him, and stayed faithful to Him throughout His ministry. Mary of Bethany was the true disciple. Listening and learning from Him, she sat at His feet and anointed Him with a pint of expensive perfume. The wealthiest of us, Mary, the mother of James, sacrificed her great wealth and her son for Jesus. And I, Mary Magdalene, stayed so dearly devoted to Jesus' ministry that I was commissioned to tell Jesus' disciples that He had risen from the dead.

Jesus blessed all us Marys by His genuine compassion, consideration of our intellectual abilities, and commendations for our ministries, worship, and devotion to Him. He never forgot us, even as He went to the tomb and rose again.

We, along with a host of nameless women, witnessed His vile death. This did not cause us to faint or desert Jesus as some of His disciples had. We Marys showed courage, kindred spirits, and faithfulness to Jesus throughout His last hours of suffering and His ascension into Heaven. We women witnesses—ones loved, recognized, and appreciated by Jesus—were granted the honor of guaranteeing to all people that Jesus still lives!

Today Jesus lives, and the powerful guarantee by the Marys keeps hope alive when we are struggling with uncertainty or healing our troubled hearts. Know that Jesus lives, inspires us, and spurs us on to deliverance and victory.

After He ascended into Heaven, Jesus did not look for a bed of ease. Instead, He got busy at the throne of God. He began to actively make intercession for our souls. He heard prayers and needs. Today, He hears us and whispers to us, "Do not be afraid. I am alive! And, I am alive from sunset to sunrise and evermore. I will always be with you—even beyond the grave."

PRAYER
Triumphant Lord, my True Vine, thank You for Your generous gift of life. Help me abide in Your presence night and day. Amen.

EXTENDED SCRIPTURES
Matthew 1:16–25, 27:55–56, 61, 28:1; Mark 3:31, 14:1–9;
Luke 1–2, 10:38–42;
John 2:1–5, 11:28–36, 45, 12:3–8, 19:25–27, 20:1–8;
Acts 1:14; Romans 16:6

BLESSING FOCUS
Female Benefactors and Women Who Leave a Legacy

VICTORY

VICTORY

SCRIPTURE
"… and I will dwell in the house of the LORD for ever."
—Psalm 23:6b

BLESSED WOMAN FOR TODAY
YOUR NAME: _____

ongratulations on completing the thirty days designed
for your enlightenment, enrichment, and encouragement. I pray
that you feel closer to God, other women, and the sons of God
more than ever before. God loves you and has prepared the best
for you.

Take a moment to acknowledge the breath of life. Inhale and
exhale. As you inhale again, breathe in the freshness of God's love.
And, as you exhale, relax, knowing that you are in God's loving
presence. His love is unconditional, all-inclusive, and unending.
He knows your desires and concerns. There is nothing too hard for
God, so continue to take everything to Him in prayer.

Women were created from life to give life. Whether giving
life through the womb, by adopting a child, spreading random
or decisive acts of kindness, using spiritual gifts, or caring for
loved ones, women are one of God's special treasures.

Wonderfully and perfectly created in the image and
likeness of God, you are being prepared to excel in service to
Him and His people. He has anointed your body and wants
you to accept His power. He wants you to stay focused on the
abiding presence of His goodness, mercy, and grace. This will
keep you abiding in His household.

As you dwell deeply with Him, you will find faith and courage to do what seems to be impossible. As you stay devoted to practicing daily prayer, you will find that you can do all through Him who strengthens you and sustains you. This wonderful life in devotion to Christ is your life now and forever.

Blessed woman, take a moment to reflect on God's blessings in your life today. Jot them down as a reminder of how God loves you and is providing for you. During the day, continue to build your awareness of God's love for you as you refer to these reminders frequently. Add more blessings to your list.

Take a moment right now, and genuinely thank God for His goodness.

Now praise Him for Who He is—all-knowing, all-powerful, providential, everywhere-present, magnificent, mighty. He is truly our awesome God, and He's yours.

LET'S PRAY TOGETHER

Loving Lord, our Provider, Protector, and Prince of Peace, thank You for Your everlasting love. Thank You for drawing us closer to You. Help us to continue to listen to Your voice each morning and throughout the day. Lead us to Your Word to deepen and enrich our relationship with You, for wherever we are, You are with us. Help us to continue to praise You. You continue to make us more beautiful, more bountiful, and more wonderful every day. Our souls rejoice in Your marvelous works; in Jesus' name. Amen.

EXTENDED SCRIPTURES
1 Corinthians 10:13; Hebrews 10:39, 13:20–21; Philippians 4:13

BLESSING FOCUS
Women in the Arts and
_____ *(your name)*

VICTORY

Taste and see that the LORD is good. Oh, the joys [and blessings] of those who trust in Him!

—Psalm 34:8, NLT

THE BLESSED WOMAN'S PRAYER

*Precious Lord, Provider, Protector, and Lover of my soul,
You are marvelous, mighty, and masterful. You see all, know all, and
are All in all. I adore You and worship You. I praise Your name for new
mercies every day.*

*Thank You for interceding for my good. Fend for me and guard me
from unseen enemies, terrorists, and the works of the devil. Do not
leave me in any temptation. Prosper me with Your perfect plan for my
peace, comfort, joy, and radiant life.*

*Help me to surrender—totally and completely—to Your will. As I
obey, help me go deeper in Your peace when I feel pain and deeper in
Your faith when I am in fear. Help me go deeper in Your comfort when
I am confused and deeper in Your strength when I feel helpless. And help
me go deeper in Your love when I am lonely. Uplift me with Your joy.*

*As You restore my soul, hold me in Your arms of mercy. See me
through Your eyes of grace and hear me through Your ears of forgiveness.
As the Holy Spirit touches my spirit, my heart glows with gladness. The
cup of my life overflows with good fortune.*

*Now order my steps by the direction of Your Word. I will entrust
my desires, dreams, and destiny to Your wisdom. You are my anchor,
shelter, and secret place in all circumstances. As You bless me, make me
bless others.*

*Resting on Your promises and in Your everlasting arms keeps me
calm, confident, and courageous. I glorify Your wonderful name and
dwell in Your loving presence forever.*

Amen.

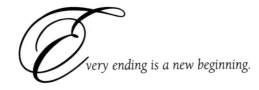

very ending is a new beginning.

My Journal of praise, answered prayer, thanksgiving,
treasured thoughts, new ideas...

....
....
....
....
....
....
....
....
....
....
....
....
....
....
....
....
....
....
....
....

About the Author

Dr. Martis Marie Jones, best-selling author, "encouragement" keynote speaker, and church minister, is best known for touching the hearts and souls of thousands through the Word of God. Her God-inspired messages of hope, deliverance, and victory help thousands discover peace, joy, and radiant life.

Believing God's call on her life to serve others through His Word, Dr. Jones turned from twenty years as a corporate executive and successful business owner to the ministry. She has never been disappointed in her obedience to God's will. Today, through her unique ministry, she reveals her divinely inspired message: "Within every disappointment grows a seed for deliverance and victory." As she edifies through this truth, she combines a God-inspired mix of sensitivity to others, humility, and practicality.

Recognized as a leader-by-example in women's ministry, discipleship, evangelism, and church leadership around America, Dr. Jones is a living testimony of God's grace. She did not grow her perpetual passion for devotion and excellence from popular panaceas or quick fixes. She was tested and tried firsthand through ten tough years when she went from "having it all" to "losing it all." However, God's amazing grace saved Dr. Jones when she did not know how to save herself. He delivered her through His divine love and ushered her to victory. Her victory songs herald the joy and power in God's Word and portray how she triumphed in turning her daunting stones of discouragement and despair into a new lifestyle, more directed from the Holy Spirit within than destructive outer circumstances.

Today, a proven, dedicated, and skilled church leader, Dr. Jones is senior minister of EdenNOW Ministries. With urgency for suffering souls, Dr. Jones stays on the cutting edge of spirit-filled living and holds the distinction for guiding women to the ecstasy in victorious living.

When Dr. Jones is not preaching from church pulpits, presenting from conference platforms, or working directly with diverse groups and individuals, she can be found talking about God's goodness on radio and television or writing Christian materials. Among her other books of encouragement, *The Prodigal Principle,* a bestseller about managing personal and professional change, wins praise from readers around the globe.

Dr. Jones holds a doctorate from Vanderbilt University and resides in Kansas City, Missouri. She is blessed with two college-age sons.

To contact the author write:
    EdenNOW Ministries
    P.O. Box 788
    Lee's Summit, MO 64063-0788
    Or e-mail: Backtoedennow@aol.com

Dr. Jones welcomes your testimony, statements on help received from this book, or prayer requests.

To Order Additional Copies

SEND $12.95* plus $4.95
for shipping and
handling to:

WinePress Publishing
P. O. Box 428
Enumclaw, WA 98022

or have your credit card
ready and call:

1-877-421-READ
(1-877-421-7323)
24 hours daily

or order online at:
www.winepresspub.com

The author and EdenNOW Ministries will donate one
dollar for each book sold to authorized, nonprofit
organizations and faith-based initiatives that service the
needs of underprivileged and abused women and children.

For information on how to share in fundraising activities
to support authorized women's organizations and churches,
e-mail EdenNOW Ministries at Backtoedennow@aol.com.

*Quantity discounts available